THE GREAT BOOK OF ANIMAL KNOWLEDGE

GRIZZLY BEARS

Humpbacked Giants of North America

All Rights Reserved. All written content in this book may NOT be reproduced in any form or by any means, including scanning, photocopying, or otherwise without prior written permission of the copyright holder. Copyright © 2014

Some Rights Reserved. All photographs contained in this book are under the Creative Commons license and can be copied and redistributed in any medium or format for any purpose, even commercially. However, you must give appropriate credit, provide a link to the license, and indicate if changes were made.

Introduction

The grizzly bear, also called the grizzly, is a type of brown bear. Grizzly bears are different from brown bears in that their fur has white tips. They were called grizzly bears because the white tip in their fur made them look like they were grizzled.

What Grizzly Bears Look Like

Photo by chascar (flickr.com/chascar), as licensed under CC BY 2.0 Generic

Grizzly bears have a hump on their shoulders made out of pure muscles. They also have steep sloped foreheads leading into a muzzle, and small rounded ears. Their tails are short and snuck to their body, so it's hard to see it. Their fur is usually colored dark brown, but they can also be light cream colored or even black.

Height and Weight

Photo by Sharon Mollerus (flickr.com/clairity), as licensed under CC BY 2.0 Generic

Grizzly Bears are very tall animals. They reach 7 feet tall when they stand upright and 4 feet, from their shoulders, when they stand on all fours! Male grizzly bears are heavier than female grizzly bears, weighing up to 600 pounds, while the females only weigh 400 pounds.

Fur

The grizzly bears got their name because of their long guard hairs at their backs and shoulders which have white tips, giving the bear a grizzled look. Their thick fur is used for protecting the bear from insects. And the brown color is used for blending them into their surroundings.

Senses

Grizzly bears have excellent senses of smelling and hearing, but their eyesight is not so good because of their forward, tiny, and closely spaced eyes. Their eyesight can be compared to that of human's eyesight. Grizzlies use smell to find food and avoid enemies. Their sense of hearing is also helpful in finding prey.

Athletics

Photo by Carl Chapman (flickr.com/carlchapman), as licensed under CC BY-SA 2.0 Generic

Despite their size, grizzlies are actually very athletic. They are very good swimmers. They are not fast swimmers, though, but still, they are very comfortable in water. Grizzlies can also climb trees using their long claws, powerful hind legs, and the hump on their shoulders. As if those aren't athletic enough, they are also very fast runners.

Behavior

People think bears are very aggressive and will attack humans at sight, but that is not true. Actually grizzly bears try to avoid humans. However, they will attack if you surprise, annoy, or scare them, or if a mother is being protective of her cub. But try to avoid bears at all times, because you never really know when they will attack.

What Grizzly Bears Eat

Photo by Carl Chapman (flickr.com/carlchapman), as licensed under CC BY-SA 2.0 Generic

Grizzlies are omnivorous, meaning they eat both plants and meat. Plant foods take up most of the grizzlies' diet, because of the plants easy access. They also eat insects, fish, and newborn moose, elk, or deer. They eat fruits, as well.

Hunting

Photo by Carl Chapman (flickr.com/carlchapman), as licensed under CC BY-SA 2.0 Generic

They use their long claws and muscled shoulders to dig the ground for insects or roots. When they hunt for fish, grizzlies will stand in the water and put their muzzles inside the water and grab a fish. Hunting for newborn moose, elk, and deer is more difficult. They chase the deer family and hope a newborn will be left behind.

What Grizzly Bears Do

The grizzlies' daily activities depend on the seasons. During winter, they stay in a den and sleep throughout the whole winter season. In spring, they spend the day and night eating to nourish themselves after one season without eating. They hardly sleep in the spring. When summer arrives, they don't eat so much, and even spend the mornings and afternoons napping. In the first half of autumn, grizzlies will eat as much as they can to prepare for their hibernation in the winter. In late autumn, they start searching for a den where they can sleep in the winter season. They hardly sleep throughout autumn.

Where Grizzly Bears Live

Grizzly bears are found in many different habitats, from thick forests to meadows, open plains, and arctic tundra. Grizzly bears are found only in North America. They can be found in western Canada, Alaska, Wyoming, Montana, Idaho, and a small population in Washington.

Territory

Photo by Gregory "Slobirdr" Smith (flickr.com/slobirdr), as licensed under CC BY-SA 2.0 Generic

Grizzly bears live by themselves, except when female grizzlies are taking care of their cubs or on mating season. Even if they live alone, they can tolerate each other; groups of grizzlies even feed together in places with plenty of food, like salmon streams. However, they have their own territories where they don't allow other grizzlies to enter.

Communication

Photo by Cynthia Heath (flickr.com/fresianrose), as licensed under CC BY 2.0 Generic

Grizzlies communicate more with body language and scent rather than with sound. Moaning, grunting, and growling are some ways they communicate through sound. Posture and movement are crucial to the grizzly bear's communication. How a grizzly is standing, moving, or behaving can provide a clear sign of the grizzlies' plan. One way of scent communication is through tree rubbing, this, however, is only done by males. When they rub the tree, their scent will be left behind and will tell other grizzlies that that place is already taken.

Hibernation

Grizzly bears hibernate throughout the winter. However, unlike other animals that hibernate, grizzlies are not always asleep and even sometimes go out of their den to find some food. And they are also easily awakened from a deep sleep when they hear movements close to their den. But most of the winter they are in their dens, sleeping.

Breeding

May and June are the grizzly bears' mating season. However, female grizzlies will only become pregnant when they start hibernating, that could be 6 months after the actual mating. If she doesn't have enough food to sustain her body while hibernating, then she won't become pregnant. Pregnancy for the grizzly bear is short. About half way through her hibernation she gives birth.

Baby Grizzly Bears

A female grizzly gives birth to about 1 to 4 cubs. The cubs are born blind and without fur and teeth. They are also born very tiny. Throughout the whole winter, they just stay close to their mother, drinking her milk. When hibernation season ends, the cubs have opened their eyes, grown their fur and teeth, and are stronger. The new family is now ready to go out of their den.

Life of a Grizzly Bear

Cubs stop drinking milk from their mother when they're 1 year old. Their mother teaches them all they need to know until they reach the age of 3. At 3 years old, the cubs then go their separate ways from their mother and each other; however, female grizzly cubs tend to make their territories beside their mothers. Female grizzlies can start mating at 5 years old while males start when they are 7.

Grizzlies can live for up to 15 to 20 years old.

Predators

Because of their size and strength, adult grizzlies don't have any natural predators. However, the cubs are very in danger against wolves, mountain lions, and even male grizzly bears. The mother will try to protect her cub by fighting against the predators when they come close to her cubs. And so that makes the mother grizzly in danger also.

Threats

Grizzly bears are now endangered, meaning there are only a few of them left. They are endangered because of several reasons. First reason is because of their slow reproduction rate. And also, half the cubs that are born don't survive the first year. They die either by getting killed, diseases, or starvation. Grizzlies are also endangered because of habitat loss, due to the cutting down of forests, etc., and getting hunted by people.

Black Bear

Despite difference in size and color, the black bear and the grizzly bear are quite similar. The best way to tell them apart is the size of their shoulders and the shape of their faces. The black bear has a flatter nose, larger ears, and it doesn't have a hump on its shoulders. The black bear is not only colored black, it can be colored black, blue-black, dark brown, brown, cinnamon, and even white.

Polar Bear

The polar bear lives mainly in the Arctic Circle. The polar bear is the largest kind of bear. The polar bears are also the only fully carnivorous, meat-eating, bears. What are polar bears colored? You would probably answer white. But actually, polar bears' fur is transparent and has no color. It only appears white because it reflects light. The skin of the polar bear is actually colored black! Also, polar bears do not hibernate.

Get the next book in this series!

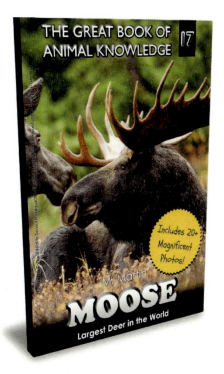

MOOSE: Largest Deer in the World

Log on to Facebook.com/GazelleCB for more info

Tip: Use the key-phrase "The Great Book of Animal Knowledge" when searching for books in this series.

For more information about our books, discounts and updates, please Like us on Facebook!

Facebook.com/GazelleCB

Made in the USA
Monee, IL
14 December 2021